ADDICTED to GOD

Jim Burns

Regal

From Gospel Light
Ventura, California, U.S.A.

D1042792

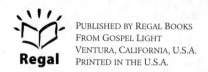

PUBLISHED BY REGAL BOOKS
FROM GOSPEL LIGHT
VENTURA, CALIFORNIA, U.S.A.
PRINTED IN THE U.S.A.

Regal Books is a ministry of Gospel Light, a Christian publisher dedicated to serving the local church. We believe God's vision for Gospel Light is to provide church leaders with biblical, user-friendly materials that will help them evangelize, disciple and minister to children, youth and families.

It is our prayer that this Regal book will help you discover biblical truth for your own life and help you meet the needs of others. May God richly bless you.

For a free catalog of resources from Regal Books/Gospel Light, please call your Christian supplier or contact us at 1-800-4-GOSPEL *or* www.regalbooks.com.

All Scripture quotations, unless otherwise indicated, are taken from the *Holy Bible, New International Version*®. Copyright © 1973, 1978, 1984 by International Bible Society. Used by permission of Zondervan Publishing House. All rights reserved.

Other versions used are
KJV—King James Version. Authorized King James Version.
NKJV—Scripture taken from the *New King James Version*. Copyright © 1979, 1980, 1982 by Thomas Nelson, Inc. Publishers. Used by permission. All rights reserved.
RSV—From the *Revised Standard Version* of the Bible, copyright 1946, 1952 and 1971 by the Division of Christian Education of National Council of the Churches of Christ in the USA. Used by permission.

© Copyright 1999 by Jim Burns. All rights reserved.
Cover design by Josh Talbot Design (www.joshtalbotdesign.com)

Formerly published by Harvest House Publishers as *Getting in Touch with God*.
First Regal Books edition, 2001.
Second edition, 2007.

Library of Congress Cataloging-in-Publication Data
Burns, Jim 1953-
  Addicted to God / Jim Burns
    p. cm.
  ISBN 0-8307-4303-0 (pbk.)
  1. Devotional calendars. I. Title.

BV4811.B835 2000
242'.2—dc21   99-047583

1   2   3   4   5   6   7   8   9   10   /   10   09   08   07

Rights for publishing this book in other languages are contracted by Gospel Light Worldwide, the international nonprofit ministry of Gospel Light. Gospel Light Worldwide also provides publishing and technical assistance to international publishers dedicated to producing Sunday School and Vacation Bible School curricula and books in the languages of the world. For additional information, visit www.gospellightworldwide.org; write to Gospel Light Worldwide, P.O. Box 3875, Ventura, CA 93006; or send an e-mail to info@gospellightworldwide.org.

To my daughter, Christy Meredith Burns:

You have brought me a deeper love and serendipity than I ever imagined possible. Your enthusiasm, spontaneity and zeal for life daily provide me with a fresh appreciation of God's goodness and faithfulness.

I can never adequately express my gratitude to God for your coming into our lives.

You are loved . . .

Agape,
Dad

Contents

Attitude

Love

Celebrate Life

God's Faithful Promises

You Are Special

Christian Adventure

Encouragement

Acknowledgments

Special thanks go to Carrie Hicks for your incredible self-less heart and your inspirational attitude. Thank you for the many extra miles you have gone for our ministry. You are making a difference. You are a most remarkable person.

A big thank-you also goes to Scott Rubin for your excellent contributions to the Going Deeper sections. I would want you as my youth worker. Thank you also for your joyful friendship and our driving-school experience.

Many, many thanks to our wonderful staff at National Institute of Youth Ministry and my friends at Gospel Light for being "difference makers."

Take the 50-Day Challenge

Authorities tell us that it takes several weeks to form a habit. Many times we talk about bad habits, but what about creating a lifelong positive habit of spending a few minutes each day with God? This book is geared to give you the opportunity to spend about 5 to 10 minutes a day with God. In just 50 short days, you will have read 50 Scriptures, experienced a short devotional and been challenged to go deeper in your relationship with our Lord. In less than two months, you can create one of the most important habits of your life. All it takes is a commitment on your part to open up this book and spend some time with God.

My experience is that thousands of students and adults are making some of the wisest decisions of their lives and are taking the 50-Day Challenge to spend the next 50 days doing regular devotional time with God. Their spiritual lives are growing and they are finding positive ways to overcome the strains and pressures of their daily lives. I encourage you to take the 50-Day Challenge and watch your relationship with God mature and strengthen. So go ahead and take the challenge, and let's watch God take up a more important part of your life.

A Resource for All Seasons

Addicted to God was created to help young people grow spiritually, but unexpectedly I have discovered this book is a powerful resource for adults, too. The stories, illustrations and quotes are invaluable in seasoning any presentation or personal study. Although the "Take the 50-Day Challenge" is a helpful way to motivate students to study the Word of God, it also offers a framework for parents, teachers, preachers and evangelists to find strength in God's daily provision as evidenced in the stories and truths collected in this book.

Addicted to God is a wonderful resource for all seasons that can be drawn upon for enriching our commitment to Christ Jesus. This devotional can be utilized in the following ways:

- Spiritual growth material for camps and retreats
- Illustrations for talks
- One-on-one or small-group devotions
- Personal studies

- Family discussions
- Stories and tales for Sunday School
- Sermon material for church worship

Many of these daily devotionals are some of my favorite illustrations from the lives and writings of others. Thank you for adding this book to your spiritual tool kit of resources, because I am confident you will find *Addicted to God* an invaluable companion in helping young people grow in Christ's wisdom and grace and in challenging adults to grow in the Lord's love and good deeds.

Attitude

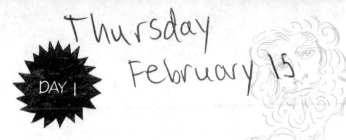

An Attitude of Thankfulness

Give thanks in all circumstances, for this is God's
will for you in Christ Jesus.

1 Thessalonians 5:18

There is always reason to be thankful. Notice that today's Scripture doesn't say to be thankful *for* all things but to be thankful *in* all things. Even in the most difficult of circumstances, you can find a reason for a thankful heart. I like the phrase that says, "I complained because I had no shoes until I met a man who had no feet." No matter what your circumstances, I believe there is a reason to be thankful in your circumstances. Your situation may never change, but your attitude can change, and that will make all the difference in the world.

Terry Foxe was a Canadian distance runner who started a run from one side of Canada to the other. He ran at least 26 miles a day to raise money for cancer research. He was a cancer victim himself. He ran every mile on one leg, since his right leg had been amputated well above the knee. Almost every day a television announcer or radio newscaster would put a microphone in front of Terry and ask him how his run for cancer was going. Often exhausted and losing valuable strength, Terry would say, "I don't know about tomorrow, but God gave me another day to live, and I'm thankful for each day I'm alive."

Terry didn't finish his run across Canada, because he died of the dreaded disease. Yet even to the end, he remained thankful for each day and considered each day God's gift to him. With an attitude of thankfulness he made the most of a difficult situation.

Going Deeper

1. What is the difference between being thankful *for* all circumstances and being thankful *in* all circumstances as is prescribed in 1 Thessalonians 5:18?

2. What are your circumstances right now? Is it time for you to begin developing a greater attitude of thankfulness in your life?

Further Reading: 1 Chronicles 16:8; Psalm 136:1.

Joy Is Yours

Rejoice in the Lord always. I will say it again: Rejoice!

Philippians 4:4

Did you know that over 500 times in the Bible we are commanded to rejoice? According to *The Living Bible,* "Be full of joy." Every morning I repeat to myself a particular verse in the psalms. In fact some mornings I say it while looking in the mirror, because I don't feel joyful. Nevertheless this verse is forever true and always helpful. Here it is:

> This is the day the Lord has made; let us rejoice
> and be glad in it (Psalm 118:24).

The truth of that psalm helps me get my day started on the right track. I have found that if I start my day rejoicing in the Lord, my day will be full of joy. A great preacher once said, "The surest mark of a Christian is not faith or even love, but joy." Did you know that Jesus came to give you joy, a deep, overflowing joy that only comes from God? Jesus said, "I have told you this so that my joy may be in you and that your joy may be complete" (John 15:11).

God's kind of joy is not a giddy, superficial good feeling. Rather, His joy runs deep. Even during the tough times, it prevails in your soul.

Going Deeper

1. Why do you think the writer of Philippians repeats himself in verse 4:4?
2. Have you ever felt peace or hope in the midst of trials? If you have, then you have experienced joy. What do you think is the connection between rejoicing in the Lord and being filled with joy?

*The Lord brings joy &
when we rejoice in him he
will fill us with joy.*

Further Reading: Romans 12:12; Philippians 3:1.

Your Attitude Makes the Difference

I will bless the Lord at all times;
his praise shall continually be in my mouth.
My soul makes its boast in the Lord; let the afflicted hear and be glad.
O magnify the Lord with me, and let us exult his name together!
I sought the Lord, and he answered me,
and delivered me from all my fears.
Look to him, and be radiant; so your faces shall never be ashamed.
This poor man cried, and the Lord heard him,
and saved him out of all his troubles.

Psalm 34:1-6, RSV

There were once two men, Mr. Wilson and Mr. Thompson, both seriously ill in the same room of a great hospital, quite a small room, just large enough for a pair of them: two beds, two bedside lockers, a door opening on the hall and one window looking out on the world.

As part of his treatment, Mr. Wilson was allowed to sit up in bed for an hour in the afternoon (something to do with draining the fluid from his lungs). His bed was next to the window. But Mr. Thompson had to spend all of his time flat on his back. Both of them had to be kept quiet and still, which was the reason they were in the small room themselves, though they were grateful for the peace and privacy. None of the bustle and clatter and prying eyes of the general ward for them. Of course, one of the disadvantages of their condition was that they weren't allowed to do much: no reading, no radio, certainly no television. They just had to keep quiet and still, just the two of them.

Well, they used to talk for hours and hours about their wives, children, homes, jobs, hobbies, childhood, what they did during the war, where they'd been on vacations, all that sort of thing. Every afternoon, when Mr. Wilson, the man by the window, was propped up for his hour, he would pass the time by describing what he could see outside. And Mr. Thompson began to live for those hours.

The window apparently overlooked a park with a lake where there were ducks and swans, children throwing them bread and sailing model boats, and young lovers walking hand in hand beneath the trees. And there were flowers and stretches of grass, games of softball, people taking their ease in the sunshine, and right at the back, behind the fringe of trees, there was a fine view of the city skyline. Mr. Thompson would listen to all of this, enjoying every minute—how a child nearly fell into the lake, how beautiful the girls were in their summer dresses, then an exciting ball game or a boy playing with his puppy. It got so that he could almost see what was happening outside.

Then one fine afternoon when there was some sort of parade, the thought struck him: *Why should Wilson, next to the window, have all the pleasure of seeing what was going on? Why shouldn't I get the chance?* He felt ashamed and tried not to think like that, but the more he tried, the more he wanted a change. He would do anything! In a few days he had turned sour. *He* should be by the window. He brooded. He couldn't sleep and grew even more seriously ill, which the doctors just couldn't understand.

One night as he stared at the ceiling, Mr. Wilson suddenly woke up, coughing and choking, the fluid congesting in his lungs, his hands groping for the call button that would bring the night nurse running. But Mr. Thompson watched without moving. The coughing racked the darkness. On and on. Mr. Wilson choked and then stopped. The sound of breathing stopped. Mr. Thompson continued to stare at the ceiling.

In the morning, the day nurse came in with water for their baths and found Mr. Wilson dead. They took his body away quietly, with no fuss.

As soon as it seemed decent, Mr. Thompson asked if he could be moved to the bed next to the window. So they moved him, tucked him in, made him quite comfortable and left him alone to be quiet and still. The minute they'd gone, he propped himself up on one elbow, painfully and laboriously, and strained as he looked out the window.

It faced a blank wall.[1]

Your attitude makes all the difference in the world. Some people face a blank wall and see dry, chipped paint while others see beautiful opportunities and numerous possibilities. How is your attitude today? In Jesus Christ you have hope. In Jesus Christ you have the knowledge that although all is not a bed of roses, God reigns and is victorious.

With the good news of Jesus, your attitude can be positive, healthy, vibrant and filled with *joy*.

Because of God's goodness, you can look toward a bright and glorious tomorrow. You can truly say, "I will bless the Lord at all times; his praise shall continually be in my mouth."

Going Deeper

1. What is the attitude of the psalmist in Psalm 34:1-6? joyful
2. Take an attitude check today. What in your life could use a change of attitude?

   School, people, family, friends.

Further Reading: Psalms 25:3; 36:9; 71:6; 1 Corinthians 1:31; Ephesians 5:20.

There Is a Season

Rejoice with those who rejoice; mourn with those who mourn.

Romans 12:15

One of the important characteristics of a servant of God is the ability to rejoice with those who rejoice and weep with those who weep. Sometimes we let envy get in the way of rejoicing in other people's success. Are you the type of person who can put your own emotions and troubles aside in order to get into the feelings of your friends who need you? Jesus had the ability to celebrate with friends at a wedding party and mourn with those at the death of a loved one.

Life tends to go in circles. We must learn the meaning of these words taken from the book of Ecclesiastes:

To everything there is a season,
A time for every purpose under heaven:
A time to be born, and a time to die;
A time to plant, and a time to pluck what is planted . . .
A time to weep, and a time to laugh . . .
A time to embrace, and a time to refrain from embracing . . .
A time to keep silence, and a time to speak;

A time to love, and a time to hate;
A time of war, and a time of peace.
Ecclesiastes 3:1-8, *NKJV*

When you learn this truth, you'll learn one of the most important lessons of life: "To everything there is a season, [and] a time for every purpose under heaven."

Going Deeper

1. What season of life described in Ecclesiastes 3:1-8 have you experienced? Who was there to help you celebrate or mourn during these seasons? *parents, family, friends*

2. Do you have the ability to come alongside people who are mourning and mourn with them? What steps can you take to make this characteristic a stronger part of your life?

Think of what Jesus would do in that situation.

Further Reading: Ecclesiastes 8:6; Amos 5:13.

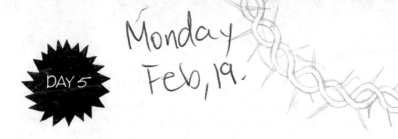

Monday
Feb, 19.

Thankful People
Are Happy People

Give thanks to the God of heaven.
His love endures forever.

Psalm 136:26

A few years ago a woman was standing on top of a 54-story building in New York City. She was ready to jump to her death and the police suicide squad was taking her extremely seriously. She didn't look the type with her expensive dress and distinguished appearance, but regardless of her appearance, every attempt to convince her to get down from the ledge ended in failure.

One of the police officers called his pastor to pray. His pastor said he would come right over and see if he could help. When this wise minister appraised the situation, he asked the captain if he might try to get close enough to talk with the woman. The captain shrugged and said, "What do we have to lose?"

The pastor started walking toward her, but she screamed as before, "Don't come any closer or I'll jump!"

He took a step backward and called out to her, "I'm sorry you believe no one loves you!" This got her attention and also the attention of the suicide squad because it was so unorthodox. The pastor went on to say, "Your grandchildren must never have given you any attention."

At this statement she took a step toward him and emphatically replied, "My family loves me and my grandchildren are wonderful. I have eight grandchildren."

The pastor took a step toward her and said, "But you must be very poor to be so desperate to jump."

She looked at her plump body and very nice dress and said, "Do I look like I'm in need of a meal? We live near Central Park in a beautiful apartment."

The pastor took another step and was now within three feet of her. He asked, "Then why do you want to jump and kill yourself?"

She surprisingly replied, "I don't remember."

This pastor had helped turn her focus off her problems and onto reasons to be thankful. They continued to talk while she showed him pictures of her eight grandchildren and gave him lengthy descriptions of each family member! A year later she was a volunteer on a suicide-prevention hot line, helping people not only to choose life but also to choose the thankful life. She had learned the secret that thankful people are happy people.

Going Deeper

1. What reason does Psalm 136:26 give us to be thankful? *For God's love*

2. Start your day with a few minutes of giving thanks to God. Try writing down the things you are thankful for and share them with your friends and family.

   · Home
   · Family
   · Certain friends
   · Church
   · College

Further Reading: Psalms 100:4; 107:1.

Garbage In, Garbage Out

Whatever is true, whatever is noble, whatever is right,
whatever is pure, whatever is lovely, whatever is admirable—
if anything is excellent or praiseworthy—think about such things.

Philippians 4:8

There's a simple principle that says when you put garbage into your mind and life, garbage will come out. When you put good things into your mind and life, then good things will flow out. Your mind matters, and what you put into your mind will ultimately make the difference between peace or distraction.

Today, take a few minutes to follow the advice of Paul and think about what is true, noble, right, pure, lovely, admirable, excellent and praiseworthy. God's promise to you in verse 9 is that when you think of these things, the "God of peace will be with you."

People of peace are people who have learned with God's help to control their minds. They regulate what goes in, and peace prevails. Others choose to put garbage into their mind, and garbage naturally comes out.

Your mind is a powerful source of help and positive energy. Give your mind and thoughts over to God's power and you'll begin to think the thoughts of our Lord and live with the peace from above. Don't waste your precious life with less than what God has to offer. Heed this advice from Romans 12:2:

Do not conform any longer to the pattern of this world, but be transformed by the renewing of your mind. Then you will be able to test and approve what God's will is— his good, pleasing and perfect will.

Going Deeper

1. How can you apply Philippians 4:8 and Romans 12:2 to your life today? Let God take over
2. Make a plan for the area you need to work on, and ask God for His help as you claim His promise for peace in your soul.

Further Reading: Ephesians 4:23; 5:17; 1 John 2:15.

Count Your Blessings

Know that the Lord is God. It is he who made us, and we are his;
we are his people, the sheep of his pasture.
Enter his gates with thanksgiving and his courts with praise;
give thanks to him and praise his name.
For the Lord is good and his love endures forever;
his faithfulness continues through all generations.

Psalm 100:3-5

Sometimes we get so preoccupied with our problems and struggles that we forget to count our blessings. Sometimes we have to get outside ourselves and remember to ask questions such as, *What would a blind person give to see the pleasant rivers, meadows and flowers that I enjoy daily?*

Today, look at the world through the eyes of a person who has received great blessings from God. As you look upon your blessings, pause to give God praise for His mighty works. When I'm feeling low, I often take a few minutes to jot down in my journal or on a piece of paper at least 20 blessings from God. My attitude always changes when I remember to count my blessings!

Going Deeper

1. Reread Psalm 100:3-5. From this passage, what do you learn about who God is? He is Lord

2. Sometime today, literally count your blessings. Take out a sheet of paper and write down at least 20 blessings in your life. I guarantee that it will change your perspective on your day!

Further Reading: Psalms 46:10; 116:17; Ezekiel 34:31.

Love

DAY 8

Thursday
Feb 22 22

Love Is the Great Transformer

These three remain: faith, hope and love.
But the greatest of these is love.

1 Corinthians 13:13

Paul wrote to his fellow Christians in Corinth, "No eye has seen, no ear has heard, no mind has conceived what God has prepared for those who love him" (1 Corinthians 2:9). There is no one in this world who can be in love with God and remain the same. Someone sent me a card that said,

LOVE is the Great Transformer . . .
LOVE transforms:
Ambition into aspiration,
Greed into gratitude,
Selfishness into service,
Getting into giving,
Demands into dedication,
Loneliness into happiness.

Love transforms you into a person who exhibits more of the qualities of Jesus Christ. Dedicate your life to love.

Don't let our culture cheapen the meaning and transformation that takes place with *agape* love, God's highest form of love. When you seek the higher level of love, you can rest assured that your life will never be the same.

Going Deeper

1. According to 1 Corinthians 13:13, when all is said and done, what three things remain? faith, hope & love

2. Why do you think love is described as the greatest quality? What area of your life could use some transformation through love? How has the love of God shaped your life in a more positive direction? B/c it has the greatest power. Love for my enemies. To live for Him in the good & bad times.

Further Reading: 1 Corinthians 16:14; Galatians 5:5-6.

God Loves You Just the Way You Are

We love because he first loved us.

1 John 4:19

Once upon a time there was a young girl named Susie. She was a beautiful little girl with the most wonderful doll collection in the world. Her father traveled all over the world on business, and for nearly 12 years he had brought dolls home to Susie. In her bedroom she had shelves of dolls from all over the United States and from every continent on Earth. She had dolls that could sing and dance and do just about anything a doll could possibly do.

One day one of her father's business acquaintances came to visit. At dinner he asked Susie about her wonderful doll collection. After dinner Susie took him by the hand and showed him these marvelous dolls from all over the world. He was very impressed. After he took the "grand tour" and was introduced to many of the beautiful dolls, he asked Susie, "With all these precious dolls, you must have one that is your favorite. Which one is it?"

Without a moment's hesitation Susie went over to her old beat-up toy box and started pulling out toys. From the bottom of the box she pulled out one of the most ragged dolls you have ever seen. There were only a few strands of hair left on the head. The clothing had long since disappeared. The doll was filthy from many years of play outside. One of the buttons for the eyes was hanging down with only a string to keep it connected. Stuffing was coming out at the elbows and knees. Susie handed the doll to the gentleman and said, "This doll is my favorite."

The man was shocked and asked, "Why is this doll your favorite when you have all these beautiful dolls in your room?" She replied, "If I didn't love this doll, nobody would!"

That single remark moved the businessman to tears. It was such a simple statement, yet so profound. The little girl loved her doll unconditionally. She loved the doll not for its beauty or abilities but simply because it was her very own doll.[2]

God loves you the way Susie loved her doll. God loves you not for what you do but for who you are. You never need to earn God's love. He loves you because you are His special creation, and by God's unconditional love you are free to blossom into all He wants you to be. His love has no strings attached.

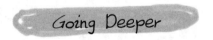

Going Deeper

1. According to 1 John 4:19, what is our motivation to love? His love

2. How do you feel when you comprehend God's
    unconditional love for you? Take a moment to
    give Him your praise and thanksgiving for His
    gracious, never-ending, never-fading love for
    you. I don't think it is possible.

Further Reading: 1 John 4:10.

Spread Your Love Around

If I speak in the tongues of men and of angels,
but have not love,
I am only a resounding gong or a clanging cymbal.
If I have the gift of prophecy and can fathom
all mysteries and all knowledge,
and if I have a faith that can move mountains,
but have not love, I am nothing.
If I give all I possess to the poor
and surrender my body to the flames,
but have not love,
I gain nothing.

1 Corinthians 13:1-3

Sometimes I feel like I can't do much to serve God or help my family and friends. But about the time I feel helpless, God reminds me that the greatest gift I can give to other people is me! People respond to love. People respond when you share your life with them. Today I want to offer you a beautiful thought about sharing.

There isn't much that I can do,
but I can share my bread with you,
and sometimes share a sorrow, too,
as on our way we go.

There isn't much that I can do,
but I can sit an hour with you,
and I can share a joke with you,
and sometimes share reverses, too,
as on our way we go.

There isn't much that I can do,
but I can share my flowers with you,
and I can share my books with you,
and sometimes share your burdens, too,
as on our way we go.

There isn't much that I can do,
but I can share my songs with you,
and I can share my mirth with you,
and sometimes come and laugh with you
as on our way we go.

There isn't much that I can do,
but I can share my hopes with you,
and I can share my fears with you,
and sometimes shed some tears with you
as on our way we go.

There isn't much that I can do,
but I can share my friends with you,
and I can share my life with you,
and oftentimes share a prayer with you
as on our way we go.[3]

Going Deeper

1. Underline the following two phrases in today's
   verse: "I am nothing" and "I gain nothing." In
   God's view how important is love? *Almost the most*
   important

2. With whom can you share your life today? What
   practical things can you do for them to let them
   know you care? You may start just by telling
   them that you love them! *Friends*

   who need love. Give w/o
   wanting anything in return.

Further Reading: Matthew 17:20; 1 Corinthians 12:9; 13:2.

Love Makes the Difference

A new commandment I give you: Love one another.
As I have loved you, so you must love one another.
By this all men will know that you are my disciples,
if you love one another.

John 13:34-35

As you look at today's Scripture, think of it in this way:
The non-Christian world has the right to judge whether or
not there is a God by the way we Christians love each other.

Yes, the world will know us by our fruit. There is no
greater witness of God's love on Earth than when Christians love in the same manner as Jesus loves.

Here is how historian Aristides described the Christians
to the Roman Emperor Hadrian:

> They love one another. They never fail to help wid-
> ows; they save orphans from those who would hurt
> them. If they have something, they give freely to the
> man who has nothing; if they see a stranger, they
> take him home, and are happy, as though he were a

real brother. They don't consider themselves brothers in the usual sense, but brothers instead through the Spirit, in God.[4]

Aristides was describing the kingdom of God made visible by believers. One of the major duties of every Christian is to make the invisible kingdom of God visible.

Going Deeper

1. What will your love for others tell people about you? Why does Jesus make loving one another a commandment? who loves me, b/c it is important

2. Think about this question: If you were arrested for being a Christian, would there be enough evidence to convict you? Yes

Further Reading: Leviticus 19:18; 1 Thessalonians 4:9; 1 Peter 1:22; 1 John 2:7-11; 3:11.

The Law of Love

You have heard that it was said,
"Love your neighbor and hate your enemy."
But I tell you: Love your enemies
and pray for those who persecute you,
that you may be sons of your Father in heaven.
He causes his sun to rise on the evil and the good,
and sends rain on the righteous and the unrighteous.
If you love those who love you, what reward will you get?
Are not even the tax collectors doing that?
And if you greet only your brothers,
what are you doing more than others?
Do not even pagans do that?

Matthew 5:43-47

When you choose to follow Jesus Christ, you are choosing to do things His way. He wants you to love people with His love, and this kind of love goes so far as to love even our enemies. One of the stories that were the most influential in my life describes something that happened during World War I. The story was told by an old colonel in the Austrian Army.

I was commanded to march against a little town on the Tyrol and lay siege to it. We had been meeting stubborn resistance in that part of the country, but we felt sure that we should win because all of the advantages were on our side. My confidence, however, was arrested by a remark from a prisoner we had taken. "You will never take that town," he said, "for they have an invincible leader."

"What does the fellow mean?" I inquired of one of my staff. "And who is this leader of whom he speaks?"

Nobody seemed able to answer my question, and so in case there should be some truth in the report, I doubled preparations.

As we descended through the pass in the Alps, I saw with surprise that the cattle were still grazing in the valley and that women and children (yes, and even men) were working in the fields.

Either they are not expecting us or this is a trap to catch us, I thought to myself. As we drew nearer the town we passed people on the road. They smiled and greeted us with a friendly word and then went on their way.

Finally we reached the town and clattered up the cobble paved streets, colors flying, horns sounding a challenge, arms in readiness. Women came to the windows or doorways with little babies in their arms. Some of them looked startled and held the babies closer, then went quietly on with their household tasks without panic or confusion. It was impossible to keep strict discipline and I began to feel rather foolish. My soldiers answered the questions of children and I saw one old warrior throw a kiss to a little golden-haired tot on a doorstep. "Just the size of Lisa," he muttered. Still no sign of an ambush. We rode straight to the open square which faced the town hall. Here, if anywhere, resistance surely was to be expected.

Just as I had reached the hall and my guard was drawn up at attention, an old white-haired man, who by his insignia I surmised to be the mayor, stepped forth, followed by ten men in simple peasant costume. They were all dignified and unabashed by the armed force before them—the most terrible soldiers of the great and mighty army of Austria.

He walked down the steps straight to my horse's side, and with hand extended, cried, "Welcome, brother!" One of my aides made a gesture as if to strike him down with his sword, but I saw by the face of the old mayor that this was no trick on his part. "Where are your soldiers?" I demanded.

"Soldiers? Why, don't you know we have none?" he replied in wonderment, as though I had asked, "Where are your giants?" or "Where are your dwarfs?"

"But we have come to take this town."

"Well, no one will stop you."

"Are there none here to fight?"

At this question, the old man's face lit up with a

rare smile that I will always remember. Often afterward, when engaged in bloody warfare, I would suddenly see that man's smile and somehow, I came to hate my business. His words were simple: "No, there is no one here to fight. We have chosen Christ for our Leader and He taught men another way."[5]

Going Deeper

1. In Matthew 5:43-47, what does God call us to do to our enemies and those who persecute us? *love & pray for them*

2. Is there someone who has done you wrong? Is it possible for you to pray for and try to love that person? *Mrs. Saunders. Yes,*

Further Reading: Leviticus 19:18; Luke 6:27,28,32.

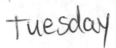

Amazing Grace

It is by grace you have been saved, through faith—and this not from yourselves, it is the gift of God—not by works, so that no one can boast.

Ephesians 2:8-9

John Newton was a slave trader and a freethinker. He lived his life opposite to what would be honoring to God. He was described as a man whose curses and lifestyle expressed his revulsion against the very idea of God's existence.

One day out at sea, the slave-trading boat that Newton was on began to break apart in an incredibly furious storm. Something snapped in Newton's mind and he remembered a verse of Scripture he had heard as a child: "If ye then, being evil, know how to give good gifts unto your children, how much more shall your Father which is in heaven give good things to them that ask him?" (Matthew 7:11, *KJV*).

"God, if this is true," Newton prayed earnestly, "make good Your Word. Cleanse my vile heart."

Four weeks later, in April 1748, the ship limped into an Irish harbor. Newton went to church and professed Jesus Christ as his Lord and Savior.

The song that best expresses his redemption is one of the most popular songs ever sung in the Christian faith:

Amazing grace! How sweet the sound
That saved a wretch like me!
I once was lost, but now am found;
Was blind, but now I see.

'Twas grace that taught my heart to fear,
And grace my fears relieved;
How precious did that grace appear
The hour I first believed!

Through many dangers, toils and snares,
I have already come;
'Tis grace that brought me safe thus far,
And grace will lead me home.

When we've been there ten thousand years,
Bright shining as the sun,
We've no less days to sing God's praise
Than when we'd first begun.[6]

Going Deeper

1. According to Ephesians 2:8-9, how are we saved?
   Why can't we save ourselves? Why doesn't God
   base our salvation on works? *by grace & faith, b/c it is not by works, so nobody can boast*

2. How do you feel about God after reading the
   words to the song "Amazing Grace"?
   That God is Amazing & All powerful

Further Reading: 1 Corinthians 1:29; 2 Timothy 1:9.

Sacrificial Love

God demonstrates his own love for us in this:
While we were still sinners, Christ died for us.

Romans 5:8

God's love is a sacrificial love. The famous statement of Jesus found in John 3:16 expresses this love best: "God so loved the world that he gave his one and only Son, that whoever believes in him shall not perish but have eternal life."

God allowed His only Son to suffer and die in order for you to experience an abundant life on Earth and eternal life with God.

When I look at the cross, I am reminded of the ultimate sacrifice that Jesus Christ made to demonstrate His love for me. His love was not just words; it was epitomized by a sacrificial deed with eternal consequences. I'm convinced that if you were the only person who needed the redemption of God, Jesus would still have gone to the cross just for you.

What is our proper response to this sacrificial love? We humble ourselves, make Christ our Lord and daily give Him our praise and thanksgiving for His mighty sacrifice. We never have to love God out of responsibility; instead,

we love Him simply out of response for what He has done
for us. Next time you notice a cross, pause and offer your
sincere thanks for His ultimate sacrifice of love.

Going Deeper

1. According to Romans 5:8, what was Christ willing to do to demonstrate His love for us? To die

2. Today do some research about the physical
   pain and suffering that Christ went through
   when He died for you. When you think about
   His physical pain and suffering, what is your
   response to Him?

   It was even more
   of a sacrafice. He stayed
   up on the cross for many
   hours. It was a pain we
   can't believe. He is amazing

Further Reading: John 15:13; 1 Peter 3:18.

Celebrate Life

Celebrate This Heartbeat

Brothers, I do not consider myself yet to have taken hold of it.
But one thing I do: Forgetting what is behind
and straining toward what is ahead, I press on toward the goal to win
the prize for which God has called me heavenward in Christ Jesus.

Philippians 3:13-14

I like what the psalmist wrote so long ago: "This is the day the Lord has made; let us rejoice and be glad in it" (Psalm 118:24). Each day you live is a gift from God. There will never be another today—so make the most of today. Live life to the fullest. It seems that the majority of people today are paralyzed by their past and are always looking for a brighter tomorrow while not making the most of today. I think the words of this contemporary Christian song make a lot of sense:

> I'm gonna celebrate this heartbeat
> 'Cause it just might be my last.
> Every day is a gift from the Lord on high,
> And they all go by so fast.
>
> So many people drifting in a dream,
> I only want to live the real thing.

I'm gonna celebrate this heartbeat
And keep movin' on,
Look toward tomorrow 'cause the past is gone.

If I laugh, it's no crime—
I've got great news on my mind.
It's a hope that never fades away.
Now I don't understand
All the mysteries of the Master plan,
But I'm sure the Master does,
So that's okay.[7]

Because God has promised to take care of your tomorrow, you can celebrate life to the fullest today.

Going Deeper

1. Paul tells us in today's verse to forget what is behind. What has happened in your life in the last week, month or year that you need to forget? old habits

2. What has happened or will happen in your life today that you can celebrate? If you are having a tough time thinking of something, just remember that the *God of the universe loves you.* Now that is worth celebrating! the weekend

Further Reading: Psalm 118:24; Luke 9:62; Romans 8:28; Hebrews 6:1.

Grasp the Hour

Whatever you do, whether in word or deed,
do it all in the name of the Lord Jesus,
giving thanks to God the Father through him.

Colossians 3:17

Life is a celebration. Don't postpone it. Grasp the hour!
Today is the first day of the rest of your life. Here is a list
of possibilities to make your day a brighter day.

- Seek out a forgotten friend.
- Write a love letter.
- Share a treasure.
- Encourage someone with a kind word.
- Keep a promise.
- Give to a needy cause.
- Forgive an enemy.
- Listen.
- Apologize if you were wrong.
- Try to understand.
- Read your Bible.
- Pray for your family.
- Appreciate a friend.

- Be kind and gentle.
- Laugh a little more. ✓
- Take pleasure in the beauty and wonder of the earth.[8]

Going Deeper

1. According to Colossians 3:17, almost anything we do or say can be a way of giving thanks to God through Jesus Christ. Make a decision to grasp the hour and thank God today. Put a check next to two of the suggestions above and do them today.

2. You may have spoken words or done deeds in your life that don't give thanks to God. Commit to making every word and deed today an opportunity to give God thanks.

Further Reading: Psalm 34:1; 1 Corinthians 10:31; Ephesians 5:20; 1 Peter 4:11.

Enjoy Life!

Do not be anxious about anything, but in everything, by prayer
and petition, with thanksgiving, present your requests to God.
And the peace of God, which transcends all understanding,
will guard your hearts and your minds in Christ Jesus.

Philippians 4:6-7

Sometimes I work too hard and take life too hard. Last week I noticed flowers in bloom in my backyard, and I had missed the process of blooming. Life is too short. Sometimes we need to sit back and enjoy God's gift to us. Brother Jeremiah was at the end of his life when he reflected on his many years of Christian service. I keep close to my heart these words he wrote:

> If I had my life to live over again, I'd try to make more mistakes next time. I would relax. I would limber up. I would be sillier than I have been this trip. I know of very few things I would take seriously. I would take more trips. I would climb more mountains, swim more rivers, and watch more sunsets. I would do more walking and looking. I would eat more ice cream and less beans. I would have more actual troubles and fewer imaginary ones.
>
> You see, I am one of those people who live pro-phylactically and sensibly and sanely, hour after

hour, day after day. Oh, I've had my moments, and if I had it to do over again, I'd have more of them. In fact, I'd try to have nothing else. Just moments, one after another, instead of living so many years ahead each day. I have been one of those people who never go anywhere without a thermometer, a hot water bottle, a gargle, a raincoat, aspirin and a parachute. If I had it to do over again, I would go places, do things, and travel lighter than I have.

If I had my life to live over, I would start barefooted earlier in the spring and stay that way later in the fall. I would play more. I would ride on more merry-go-rounds. I'd pick more daisies.[9]

Going Deeper

1. Reread Philippians 4:6-7. What is the result of not being anxious but presenting our requests to God through prayer and petition with thanksgiving? *your heart & mind will be guarded*

2. Sometimes we are anxious about life because we are sitting around thinking about it. What specifically can you do today to live life to the fullest? Do it today! *Get a job*

Further Reading: Matthew 6:25-34; John 14:27; Ephesians 6:18; Colossians 3:15.

Life Is Too Short For . . .

Do not worry about tomorrow, for tomorrow will worry about itself.
Each day has enough trouble of its own.

Matthew 6:34

One day when I was caught up in the tyranny of the urgent, my friend Bill McNabb sent me some thoughts entitled "Things That Life Is Too Short For." His thoughts forced me to take a look at my own life and reevaluate my priorities. Perhaps you need a dose of reality today. I'll share these special thoughts with you.

- Life is too short to nurse grudges or hurt feelings.
- It's too short to worry about getting ready for Christmas. Just let Christmas come.
- It's too short to keep all your floors shiny.
- It's too short to let a day pass without hugging your loved ones.
- It's too short not to take a nap when you need one.
- It's too short to put off Bible study.
- It's too short to give importance to whether the towels match the bathroom.

- It's too short to miss the call to worship on a Sunday morning.
- It's too short to stay indoors on a crisp fall Saturday.
- It's too short to read all the junk mail.
- It's too short not to call or write your parents (or children) regularly.
- It's too short to work at a job you hate.
- It's too short not to stop and talk to children.
- It's too short to forget to pray.
- It's too short to put off improving our relationships with people that we love.
- Life is just too short—way too short—to settle for mediocrity!

Going Deeper

1. What does Matthew 6:34 tell us not to do? *worry about tom*
2. Matthew 6:34 also tells us today will have enough trouble of its own. What difficulties will you face today? Take a moment to pray and ask God to take control of your day and any difficulties you may face.

Thoughts.

Further Reading: Philippians 4:6.

DAY 19

Making the Most of Today

This is the day the Lord has made; let us rejoice and be glad in it.

Psalm 118:24

Today you were handed from God 24 hours to live life to the fullest. That's 1,440 minutes or 86,400 seconds. Sometimes we get so busy and distracted we miss the fact that each rising sun brings new opportunities and adventures on this planet we call Earth.

God gives us one new day at a time so that we aren't distracted by the future or paralyzed by the past. Today is the first day of the rest of your life. Make the most of today. Enjoy God's gift to you. You can accomplish a great deal with each 1,440 minute in a day. Today stop and take advantage of all that God has provided for you. Here are a few suggestions:

- Tell someone how much you love him or her.
- Write a kind note to a friend.
- Stop and enjoy the sunset.
- Take 20 minutes of the 1,440 you have today and talk to God.

· Memorize this verse: "This is the day the Lord has made; let us rejoice and be glad in it" (Psalm 118:24).

Going Deeper

1. Rewrite Psalm 118:24 in your own words.
2. What attitude does Psalm 118:24 say we should try to have about each new day that God gives us?

① God made this day, so be happy.

② Rejoycing & glad

Further Reading: Psalm 70:4.

Tuesday

Your Use of Time

Thou hast made the moon to mark the seasons;
the sun knows its time for setting.

Psalm 104:19, RSV

The greatest commodity you have at your fingertips is *time*. Everyone has the same amount of time to use or waste today. The happiness in your life depends on how you use your time. Periodically I need to evaluate how I am using my time. This little paragraph helps me keep perspective:

Take time to THINK—it is the source of power.
Take time to PLAY—it is the secret of perpetual youth.
Take time to be FRIENDLY—it is the road to happiness.
Take time to LOVE—it is a God-given privilege.
Take time to READ—it is a fountain of wisdom.
Take time to PRAY—it is the greatest power on Earth.
Take time to LAUGH—it is the music of the soul.
Take time to GIVE—it is too short a day to be selfish.
Take time to WORK—it is the price of success.

Going Deeper

1. Reread Psalm 104:19. What has God created to show us the importance of time? *The Sun & Moon*

2. The paragraph above lists a number of ways you could spend your time each day. Take a few minutes to evaluate how you spend your time. Is your time divided appropriately between all of these important areas?

   No, I don't take time to be friendly, to love or give.

Further Reading: Genesis 1:14; Psalms 19:6; 74:16; Jeremiah 10:2.

What Can We Learn from Death?

Just as man is destined to die once, and after that to face judgment,
so Christ was sacrificed once to take away the sins of many people;
and he will appear a second time, not to bear sin,
but to bring salvation to those who are waiting for him.

Hebrews 9:27-28

No one likes to talk or think about death or the death of loved ones. However, there are certain facts we can learn from death:

1. We will all die.
2. Life is short, so we should make the most of each day.
3. Celebrate life daily. Live now; don't wait.
4. Walk with God, the creator and sustainer of life.

I like what Leo Buscaglia says about death and life:

Death teaches us if we want to hear—that the time is now. The time is now to pick up a telephone and call the person that you love. Death teaches us the joy of the moment. It teaches us we don't have forever. It teaches us that nothing is permanent. It teaches us to let go, there's nothing you can hang on to. And it tells us to give up expectations and let tomorrow tell its own story, because nobody knows if they'll get home tonight. To me that's a tremendous challenge. Death says "live now." Let's tell the children that.[10]

Going Deeper

1. According to Hebrews 9:27-28, what is the ultimate destiny of humankind on Earth? *To die*

2. What does this verse tell us about what Christ has done and what He will do? How does today's thought affect the way you think about life and death? *He has died 4 he will come back, It tells me that we need to embrace the day.*

Further Reading: Genesis 3:19; Psalms 90:3; 104:29; 2 Corinthians 5:10.

God's Faithful Promises

DAY 22

Thursday

He Makes Your Weakness His Strength

He said to me,
"My grace is sufficient for you,
for my power is made perfect in weakness."
Therefore I will boast all the more gladly about my weaknesses,
so that Christ's power may rest on me.

2 Corinthians 12:9

I asked God for strength that I might achieve.
I was made weak that I might learn humbly to obey.

I asked God for health that I might do great things.
I was given infirmity that I might do better things.

I asked for riches that I might be happy.
I was given poverty that I might be wise.

I asked for power that I might have the
praise of men.
I was given weakness that I might feel
the need of God.

I asked for all things that I might enjoy life.
I was given life that I might enjoy all things.

I got nothing I asked for but everything
I had hoped for...
Almost despite myself my unspoken prayers
were answered.

I am among all men most richly blessed.[11]

An unknown confederate soldier wrote these powerful words. He knew the truth of today's Scripture: It's not *what you have* but *who you know*. Paul wrote another thought about weakness that you should know about: "The foolishness of God is wiser than man's wisdom, and the weakness of God is stronger than man's strength" (1 Corinthians 1:25). Don't be afraid in your weakest moments to lean on the strong and steady arms of your Savior!

Going Deeper

1. According to 2 Corinthians 12:9, when might *when we* God's power be best displayed in our lives? *are weak*
2. What area of weakness can you trust to God today? Remember, God can turn our weaknesses into strengths. *My Fear*

Further Reading: Philippians 4:13.

Hope in the Midst of Hassles

I am convinced that neither death nor life, neither angels
nor demons, neither the present nor the future, nor any powers,
neither height nor depth, nor anything else in all creation, will be able
to separate us from the love of God that is in Christ Jesus our Lord.

Romans 8:38-39

If you read today's headlines in the newspaper, you can get pretty depressed. Yes, at times life looks pretty hopeless. But if we keep our eyes on our Lord Jesus Christ, we can have hope even in the midst of difficult circumstances. We can be comforted by Paul's words found in Romans 8:31: "If God is for us, who can be against us?" God is for you, and through His love you can find hope! Here are four reasons why you can remain hopeful in the midst of confusing circumstances:

1. Jesus Will Win the Final Victory
One day an old janitor was sitting in the gymnasium of a theological seminary reading the book of Revelation.

One of the young theologians sat down beside him and asked him, "Do you understand all the symbolism?"

The janitor replied, "No, absolutely not; but I have figured out that Jesus wins, and that's comforting to know 'cause I'm on His side."

Jesus told these words to the apostle John: "I am the Alpha and the Omega, the Beginning and the End. To him who is thirsty I will give to drink without cost from the spring of the water of life" (Revelation 21:6).

2. Jesus Sets Us Free

Jesus said, "You will know the truth, and the truth will set you free" (John 8:32). In Christ we can have hope because we have been set free from our sin. We are free to be all that God desires us to be without the constraints of our past. We can know the meaning of abundant life because of what Christ did for us on the cross.

3. There Is No Condemnation for Those in Christ

In Christ we are a new creation. Romans 8:1-2 puts it best: "There is now no condemnation for those who are in Christ Jesus, because through Christ Jesus the law of the Spirit of life set me free from the law of sin and death." Even though we deserve death and spiritual separation from God, we have new beginnings and eternal life in Jesus Christ. Talk about a reason for hope!

4. God's Love Transcends Human Understanding

Because God loves us, we are "more than conquerors" (Romans 8:37) through Christ. God loves you and wants the best for you. His love will give you hope even in the bleakest of circumstances. There is a light always shining, and the light is the love of God. In Him you can find hope.

Going Deeper

1. Reread Romans 8:38-39. What can separate us from the love of God? *Nothing*
2. Make a list of reasons why you can be hopeful in a world filled with hopeless happenings. Remember, if you are focused on Jesus Christ, He will give you great hope!

- Future   college
- Friends
- Family

Further Reading: Romans 5:8; Colossians 1:16.

Satisfaction Guaranteed

Blessed are those who hunger and thirst for righteousness,
for they shall be satisfied.

Matthew 5:6, RSV

There is a great promise in today's verse. If you hunger and thirst for righteousness, you will be satisfied. In order to be satisfied, you have to pursue righteousness with everything you have.

God wants our 100-percent effort. Why is it that I'll give my 100-percent effort on the tennis court or when planning a party, but when it comes to pursuing righteousness, sometimes I coast? When I'm not giving God my best, an empty feeling creeps into my life.

Today's promise in Matthew 5:6 challenges me to pull out the stops, roll up my sleeves and with reckless abandon dive into the arms of the Savior. If I pursue with all my heart and energy what God has placed on my heart, the result will be *satisfaction*.

I like what Charles Paul Conn wrote:

Whatever it is,
However impossible it seems,
Whatever the obstacle that lies between you and it,
If it is noble,

If it is consistent with God's kingdom,
You must hunger after it
And stretch yourself to reach it.[12]

Going Deeper

1. What promise does God give us in Matthew 5:6?
2. Pray specifically right now that God would cause you to hunger and thirst for righteousness. If you are sincere in your prayer, God will increase your desire to seek Him.

1-that we will be satisfied
2-

Further Reading: Romans 5:8.

DAY 25

He Is Always with You

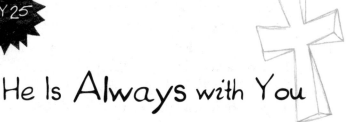

It is the LORD who goes before you;
he will be with you, he will not fail you or forsake you;
do not fear or be dismayed.

Deuteronomy 31:8, RSV

One night a man had a dream. He dreamed he was walking along the beach with the Lord. Across the sky flashed scenes from his life. For each scene he noticed two sets of footprints in the sand: one belonging to him and the other to the Lord.

When the last scene of his life flashed before him, he looked back at the footprints in the sand. He noticed that many times along the path of his life there was only one set of footprints. He also noticed that it happened at the very lowest and saddest times in his life.

This really bothered him and he questioned the Lord about it. "Lord, You said that once I decided to follow You, You'd walk with me all the way. But I have noticed that during the most troublesome times in my life, there is only one set of footprints.

I don't understand why when I needed You most You would leave me."

The Lord replied, "My precious, precious child, I love you and I would never leave you. During your times of trial and suffering, when you see only one set of footprints, it was then that I carried you."[13]

When you feel discouraged, take heart—God's promise to never leave you or forsake you is always there to get you through your troubles. Why is it that we tend to turn to Him as the last resort when He is always faithfully by our side?

Psalm 23 can be such an encouragement in times of trouble! Take a fresh look at this famous psalm and be comforted that God has walked with you through your dark days.

> The LORD is my shepherd; I shall not want.
> He maketh me to lie down in green pastures:
> he leadeth me beside the still waters.
> He restoreth my soul:
> He leadeth me in the paths of righteousness
> for his name's sake.
>
> Yea, though I walk through the valley of the
> shadow of death,
> I will fear no evil: for thou art with me;
> thy rod and thy staff they comfort me.

Thou preparest a table before me in the
presence of my enemies:
thou anointest my head with oil; my cup
runneth over.

Surely goodness and mercy shall follow
me all the days of my life:
and I will dwell in the house of the LORD
for ever (*KJV*).

Going Deeper

1. Are you ever afraid of the future? Do you ever feel lonely? Reread Deuteronomy 31:8. What does this verse do to your fears or feelings of loneliness?
2. Reread Psalm 23 and spend some time committing it to memory.

1-Yes yes, that He will be w/ us
2-

Further Reading: Exodus 13:21; 33:14.

A Reservoir of Power

You will receive power when the Holy Spirit comes on you;
and you will be my witnesses in Jerusalem,
and in all Judea and Samaria, and to the ends of the earth.

Acts 1:8

I heard a story a few years ago about a farmer in the pan-handle of Texas. This farmer and his wife had eked out a meager living in the dusty panhandle for 30 years when a man impeccably dressed in a three-piece suit and driving a fancy car came to their door. He told the farmer that he had good reason to believe there was a reservoir of oil un-derneath the farmer's property. If the farmer would allow the gentleman the right to drill, perhaps the farmer would become a wealthy man.

The farmer stated emphatically that he didn't want anyone messing up his property and asked the gentleman to leave. The next year about the same time, the gentle-man returned again with his nice clothes and another fancy car. The oilman pleaded with the farmer, and again the farmer said no.

This same experience went on for the next eight years. During those eight years the farmer and his wife really struggled to make ends meet. Nine years after the first visit from the oilman, the farmer came down with a disease that put him in the hospital. When the gentleman arrived to plead his case for oil, he spoke to the farmer's wife. Reluctantly she gave permission to drill.

Within a week, huge oil rigs began the process of drilling for oil. The first day nothing happened. The second day was filled with only disappointment and dust. But on the third day, right about noon, black bubbly liquid began to squirt up in the air. The oilman had found "black gold," and the farmer and his wife were instantly millionaires.

You have a reservoir of power in your life. If you are a Christian, the Holy Spirit works in your life. You can tap into His power and live your life with resurrection power. The Holy Spirit will empower you to live life on a greater level, but you have to tap into His power source just as the farmer needed to drill for oil. The Bible says to "be filled with the Spirit" (Ephesians 5:18) and to "live by the Spirit" (Galatians 5:16). People are searching for the power to change their lives when, in fact, the power is already dwelling within them in the form of God's Holy Spirit. Tap into His reservoir of power!

Going Deeper

1. According to Acts 1:8, what is the source of power in a Christian's life?

   The Holy Spirit

2. What is the role of the Holy Spirit in a Christian's life? If you don't know, don't be afraid to ask someone!

To live in the hearts
& minds of believers

Tuesday

Taste and See for Yourself

Delight yourself in the Lord
and he will give you the desires of your heart.

Psalm 37:4

When you've tasted all that the Lord has to offer, it is difficult to settle for rubbish. If God is our Creator and Christ is who the Bible claims Him to be, then you can come into His fullness and not be disappointed. When confronted with the truth, even skeptics who doubt the Christian faith respond to the goodness and knowledge of God.

Lew Wallace was a famous literary critic and a general during the Civil War. He believed that Christianity kept people in ignorance, fear, superstitions and bondage. One Sunday morning while riding a train, he observed hundreds of people going to Sunday worship. He decided to research and write a book that would forever liberate Christian people from their ignorance and superstitions.

For two years, Wallace studied in leading libraries of Europe and America to disclaim Christianity forever. He finished the study and began to write. He wrote his first chapter, and as he was laboring over his second chapter, he suddenly found himself on his knees saying, "My Lord and my God!" The One whom he had set out to disprove had captured him. Lew Wallace became a devout follower of Christ and authored the great Christian classic *Ben Hur: A Tale of the Christ.*

"Taste and see that the LORD is good" (Psalm 34:8).

Going Deeper

1. After reading Psalm 37:4, what do you think it means to "delight yourself in the Lord"?
2. Don't be afraid to ask questions or seek knowledge about your faith in God. As you search and experience God, you will only become more convinced of His faithfulness and reality in your life.

1- have God wf you

2-

Further Reading: Isaiah 58:14.

Hang On to Hope

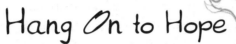

Since we are surrounded by such a great cloud of witnesses,
let us throw off everything that hinders and the sin that so easily
entangles, and let us run with perseverance the race
marked out for us.
Let us fix our eyes on Jesus, the author and perfecter of our faith,
who for the joy set before him endured the cross, scorning its shame,
and sat down at the right hand of the throne of God.

Hebrews 12:1-2

Do you ever feel like a failure? Some people look at the life of Jesus and say that He failed. He was born in obscurity. For most of His life He was a lonely carpenter. For three years He traveled as an itinerant preacher, and for those three years of effort He really didn't have many disciples and no substantial following to speak of. He died in shame with two common prisoners alongside Him. If the story stopped here, all would consider Him a failure. But the story continues, because three days later He *rose from the dead*, ascended into heaven and now sits at the right hand of our Father!

If you feel like a failure, you're in good company. Abraham Lincoln had more failures than victories, yet some would call him the greatest president the United States has ever had. Look at his life for a moment:

- He grew up on an isolated farm with only one year of formal education; in his early years he was exposed to barely half a dozen books.
- In 1832 he lost his job and was defeated in the race for the Illinois legislature.
- In 1833 he failed in business.
- In 1834 he was elected to the state legislature; but in 1835 his sweetheart died, and in 1836 he had a nervous breakdown.
- In 1838 he was defeated for Speaker of the House, and in 1843 he was defeated for nomination to Congress.
- In 1846 he was elected to Congress but in 1848 lost the renomination.
- In 1849 he was rejected for a federal land officer appointment, and in 1854 he was defeated for the Senate.
- In 1856 he was defeated for the nomination of vice president, and in 1858 was again defeated for the Senate.[14]

Was Lincoln a failure? Absolutely not! He became one of the greatest presidents in the history of the United States.

There is one word that comes to mind when I think of failure: *perseverance.* To persevere means to hang on, to stick with it, to press forward! The call of the Christian is to keep on looking to Jesus and moving in His direction. You can rest assured that Paul was right when he wrote, "He who began a good work in you will carry it on to completion until the day of Christ Jesus" (Philippians 1:6). So hang on; there is light at the end of the tunnel, and the light is the love of Christ.

Going Deeper

1. Take a deeper look at Hebrews 12:1-2. These verses tell us to throw off everything that hinders and to run with perseverance. According to this passage, what or who are we to set our eyes on? *on JESUS*

2. How does setting our eyes on Jesus help us avoid mistakes and persevere through failures?

   B/C he gets us throug the hard times

Further Reading: 1 Corinthians 9:24; Philippians 2:8-9; Hebrews 10:36.

You Are Special

DAY 29

Twsday

You Are Special

You created my inmost being;
you knit me together in my mother's womb.
I praise you because I am fearfully and wonderfully made;
your works are wonderful, I know that full well.
My frame was not hidden from you when I was made in the secret place.
When I was woven together in the depths of the earth,
your eyes saw my unformed body.
All the days ordained for me were written in your book
before one of them came to be.

Psalm 139:13-16

You are unique. You are special. God created you and there is not another person in the world exactly like you.

True, there are things about ourselves that we really don't like. (I wish I were taller, richer and more intelligent.) There are some aspects of our lives that we can work on to improve and other aspects that we must learn to accept. The people who learn to accept the good with the bad are the ones who find happiness.

Cathy and I have a prayer hanging in our bathroom that helps me when I'm feeling less than good about myself and the circumstances in my life. It simply reads:

God grant me the serenity to accept
the things I cannot change,
courage to change those I can,
and wisdom to know the difference.

Great advice for those who sometimes forget they are special in the eyes of God!

Going Deeper

1. Isn't Psalm 139:13-16 an awesome passage? Whether you like it or not, you are unique and you are special! How does this passage make you feel?

2. Is there something about how God has made you that you have been struggling to accept? Is this something that will not change or something you could change if you had the courage?

Further Reading: Psalm 119:73.

You Can Fly!

I tell you the truth, anyone who has faith in me will do what I have been doing. He will do even greater things than these, because I am going to the Father. And I will do whatever you ask in my name, so that the Son may bring glory to the Father. You may ask me for anything in my name, and I will do it.

John 14:12-14

Søren Kierkegaard tells a story about a make-believe country where only ducks live.

> On Sunday morning all the ducks came into church, waddled down the aisle, waddled into their pews, and squatted. Then the duck minister came in, took his place behind the pulpit, opened his duck Bible and read, "Ducks! You have wings, and with wings, you can fly like eagles, you can soar into the sky! Ducks! You have wings!" All the ducks yelled, "Amen!" and then they waddled home.[15]

The ducks could fly, but they settled for waddling instead. Many Christians are like those ducks: They attend church regularly and even know what the Bible has to say about living the abundant life of a committed Christian, but they never get around to acting upon their belief.

You can fly! You can soar above the clouds of mediocrity and become all that God has in store for you! Paul said, "I can do everything through him who gives me strength" (Philippians 4:13). Jesus said, "I tell you, whatever you ask for in prayer, believe that you have received it, and it will be yours" (Mark 11:24). James said, "You do not have, because you do not ask God" (James 4:2).

Has God put a dream or idea in your mind? With Christ you can accomplish that desire. You can make a difference in your world. You can fly!

Going Deeper

1. Today's Scripture informs that we have the ability to do great works for God. Do you believe this about yourself? *Yes*

2. What great things do you think God has for you to do and be?

   - Pastor?
   - Missions?
   - ~~Good~~ Father

Further Reading: Matthew 7:7; 21:21.

Never Settle for Mediocrity

I am the vine; you are the branches.
If a man remains in me and I in him, he will bear much fruit;
apart from me you can do nothing.

John 15:5

Too many people today settle for second best in life. Mediocrity is all they put into life, and mediocrity is all they get out of life. Yet Paul said, "I can do all things through Christ who strengthens me" (Philippians 4:13, *NKJV*). He doesn't sound like a person who chooses to be average, and you don't have to be average either.

There's a Native American story about a brave who found an eagle's egg and put it into the nest of a prairie chicken. The eaglet hatched with the brood of chicks and grew up with them.

All his life the changeling eagle, thinking he was a prairie chicken, did what the prairie chickens did. He scratched in the dirt for seeds and insects to eat. He clucked and cackled. And he flew in a brief thrashing of wings and flurry of feathers no more than a few feet off the ground. After all, that's how prairie chickens were supposed to fly!

Years passed, and the changeling eagle grew very old. One day he saw a magnificent bird far above him in the cloudless sky. Hanging with graceful majesty on the powerful wind currents, it soared with scarcely a beat of its strong golden wings.

"What a beautiful bird!" said the changeling eagle to his neighbor. "What is it?"

"That's an eagle—the chief of the birds," the neighbor clucked. "But don't give it a second thought. You could never be like him."

So the changeling eagle never gave it another thought. And it died thinking it was a prairie chicken.[16]

Going Deeper

1. According to John 15:5, how much fruit will a person's life bear when that person remains in Jesus? What does John mean by "fruit"?

2. Sometimes our circumstances cause us to settle for second best in life. Commit to God right now to be open to all He has in store for your life.

1. much? fruit of the spirit
2.

Further Reading: John 15:16; Galatians 5:22.

Sunday

God Draws Out the Best in You

Just as you received Christ Jesus as Lord, continue to live in him.

Colossians 2:6

Jesus had the power to draw out the best in people. He met a clumsy, big-mouthed fisherman named Simon. Jesus looked beyond Simon's present abilities to his potential. He looked Simon straight in the eye and said, "So you are Simon the son of John?" Simon nodded. Jesus said, "You shall be called Peter."

"Peter" means "rock." Jesus nicknamed Simon Peter "The Rock." At the time, Simon Peter was anything but a rock of a person. Yet Jesus saw his potential, and this fisherman became the rock-solid leader of the Jerusalem church.

Throughout the Bible we meet different individuals who had an encounter with God and became different people. Abram became "Abraham," "the father of many." Jacob met God and became "Israel," which means "he struggles with God."

It is important for you to know that God affirms you as He affirmed Bible characters. He loves you and will draw out the best in you. He sees you not only for who you are but also for who you can be.

Going Deeper

1. Colossians 2:6 challenges us to not stop at just receiving Christ but to continue daily to live in Him. Has your decision to receive Christ as Lord changed the way you live life day to day? How?

2. Part of "living in Jesus" is giving Him your insecurities and fears and letting Him draw out the very best in you. Are you willing to let God work in your life?

1- Yes my thoughts

2- Yes

Further Reading: John 13:13; Colossians 1:10.

You Are God's Poetry

We are God's workmanship, created in Christ Jesus to do good works,
which God prepared in advance for us to do.

Ephesians 2:10

Today's Scripture verse says, "We are God's workmanship." The word "workmanship" can be translated "poetry." Have you ever thought of yourself as one of God's special works of poetry? You are His special creation. You are unique. There is no one else in the whole world quite like you. You are an unrepeatable miracle.

When I'm feeling low, I need to be reminded that I'm special in God's eyes. When I'm playing the comparison game and comparing my talent or physical appearance with those I think are better than I am, I need to be reminded that God created me to be unique. When I'm playing the "I wish" game, wishing that things were different, I need to be reminded that I am the only special poem of God made just like me.

Many people today are so hard on themselves that they miss the joy of being God's only creation made from their unique mold. People who view themselves as God's special creation are the ones who live happy and successful lives. You are His poetry, so live your life as a child of God!

Going Deeper

1. Read Ephesians 2:10 and substitute the word "poetry" for the word "workmanship." How does it make you feel to know you are God's greatest poetry or workmanship?
2. Just in case you are not convinced of how special you are, say out loud, "I am God's special poem." This may sound corny, but it's true!

1- Special
2-

Further Reading: Ephesians 4:24.

Tuesday

You Are What You Think

As he thinks in his heart, so is he.

Proverbs 23:7, NKJV

Have you ever heard of the phrase "self-fulfilling prophe-cy"? A self-fulfilling prophecy is simply the truth of today's Scripture. You become what you think yourself to be. If you *think you will fail,* you probably will. If you *think you will suc-ceed,* then most likely you will succeed.

Your mind is powerful. That's why Paul gives some ex-cellent advice to the Philippian church that is still impor-tant today:

> Finally, brothers, whatever is true, whatever is noble, whatever is right, whatever is pure, whatever is love-ly, whatever is admirable—if anything is excellent or praiseworthy—think about such things. Whatever you have learned or received or heard from me or seen in me—put it into practice. And the God of peace will be with you (Philippians 4:8-9).

I'm afraid too many people's lives are a negative, self-fulfilling prophecy when in Christ we can become so much more. This little poem has helped me focus my thoughts on Christ and on the positive side of self-fulfilling prophecy:

If you think you are beaten, you are.
If you think you dare not, you don't.
If you like to win, but think you can't,
it's almost a cinch you won't.

If you think you will lose, you are lost.
For out in the world we find
success begins with a fellow's will;
It's all in the state of mind.

For many a race is lost
ere even a step is run,
and many a coward fails
ere even his work is begun.

Think big and your deed will grow,
think small and you will fall behind.
Think that you can and you will—
It's all in the state of mind.

If you think you are outclassed, you are.
You have got to think high to rise.
You have got to be sure of yourself
before you win a prize.

Life's battles don't always go
to the stronger or faster man.
But sooner or later the man who wins
is the man who thinks he can.

Going Deeper

1. List all of the things we are to think about as found in Philippians 4:8-9.
2. Examine your thought life. How does it compare to the list you found in Philippians 4:8-9?

1- underlined words
2- not great

Further Reading: Philippians 3:17.

Guilty!

All have sinned and fall short of the glory of God.

Romans 3:23

The wages of sin is death, but the gift of God is eternal life
in Christ Jesus our Lord.

Romans 6:23

On a sunny September day a stern-faced, plainly dressed man stood on a street corner in downtown Chicago. Pedestrians hurried by on their way to lunch, shopping or business. This solemn-faced man would lift his right arm, point to the person nearest him and intone loudly the single word "*Guilty!*"

Then, without any change of expression, he would resume his stiff stance for a few minutes before repeating the same gesture again, raising his arm and pointing to another person and then pronouncing loudly that one word "*Guilty!*"

The effect that this strange man had on the people was almost eerie. People would stare at him, hesitate, look aside and then hurry away as if they had been caught. One man turned to another man and exclaimed, "But how did he know?"

Guilty! We are all guilty. We have made some major mistakes in our lives, and many minor ones; we are all guilty.

When it comes to our relationship with God, we have all sinned and fallen short of His glory. To sin means to "miss the mark" and we have all missed the mark of God's perfection.

The good news is that sin and guilt are erased in Jesus Christ. There is a scriptural principal that helps us understand the beauty of God's forgiveness of our sin and guilt. It's found in 1 John 1:9: "If we confess our sins, he is faithful and just and will forgive us our sins and purify us from all unrighteousness."

You don't have to live in the guilt of your past sins. You are forgiven. You are cleansed. Your sins are no longer remembered. Hallelujah!

Going Deeper

ALL
Death

1. According to Romans 3:23, who has sinned? OK, now according to Romans 6:23, what are the wages of sin? Go to the next question!

eternal life
confess
your sins

2. We have established that we all have sinned and that we all face death because of that sin, but what hope does the second part of Romans 6:23 offer us? How can we be freed from the guilt of sin on a daily basis in our lives according to 1 John 1:9?

Further Reading: Genesis 2:17; Romans 5:12; Galatians 6:7-8.

Christian Adventure

Thursday

Authentic Christianity

We loved you so much that we were delighted to share with
you not only the gospel of God but our lives as well,
because you had become so dear to us.

1 Thessalonians 2:8

Be authentic. Be yourself. There is no greater witness than
a person who is open and vulnerable about his or her struggles and love for God.

I don't know about you, but I can't relate to perfect people, yet there are loads of Christians running around today
who want you to think they are perfect. People who act like
they don't have problems are one of the major stumbling
blocks for friends and family becoming Christians. I like the
bumper sticker that reads, "Christians aren't perfect, they're
just forgiven."

I think the old Skin Horse gave the Velveteen Rabbit
some outstanding advice about being an authentic person. Maybe this advice is good for you as well.

The Skin Horse had lived longer in the nursery than
any of the others. He was so old that his brown coat
was bald in patches and showed the seams under-

neath, and most of the hairs on his tail had been pulled out to string bead necklaces. He was wise, for he had seen a long succession of mechanical toys arrive to boast and swagger, and by-and-by break their mainsprings and pass away, and he knew that they were only toys, and would never turn into anything else. For nursery magic is very strange and wonderful, and only those playthings that are old and wise and experienced like the Skin Horse understand all about it.

"What is REAL?" asked the Rabbit one day, when they were lying side by side near the nursery fender, before Nana came to tidy the room. "Does it mean having things that buzz inside you and a stick-out handle?"

"Real isn't how you are made," said the Skin Horse. "It's a thing that happens to you. When a child loves you for a long, long time, not just to play with, but REALLY loves you, then you become Real."

"Does it hurt?" asked the Rabbit.

"Sometimes," said the Skin Horse, for he was always truthful. "When you are Real you don't mind being hurt."

"Does it happen all at once, like being wound up," he asked, "or bit by bit?"

"It doesn't happen all at once," said the Skin Horse. "You become. It takes a long time. That's why it doesn't often happen to people who break easily, or have sharp edges, or who have to be carefully kept. Generally, by the time you are Real, most of your hair has been loved off, and your eyes drop out and you get loose in the joints and very shabby. But these things don't matter at all, because once you are Real you can't be ugly, except to people who don't understand."[17]

Going Deeper

1. What are the two things authentic Christians share according to 1 Thessalonians 2:8?
2. Have you ever pretended to be something you are not? How can you strive to be more like Jesus and be more authentic in your relationships with people around you?

1- the gospel & their lives

2- yes, break habits

Further Reading: 2 Corinthians 12:15; 1 John 3:16.

Wasted Hours or Invested Hours?

Give ear to my words, O Lord; give heed to my groaning. Hearken
to the sound of my cry, my King and my God, for to thee do I pray.
O Lord, in the morning thou dost hear my voice; in the morning
I prepare a sacrifice for thee, and watch.

Psalm 5:1-3, RSV

I'm the type of person who feels that if I'm not doing something, I'm wasting my time. Prayer has been difficult for me
at times because I feel it is getting in the way of my accom-
plishing something for the day. How wrong I am when
I have this attitude! Prayer is not wasted hours but *invested*
hours. Out of solitude comes strength; out of quiet comes
peace; out of talking and listening to the Lord comes vision.
The following poem from an unknown author is a helpful
reminder of what I am talking about:

> I wasted an hour one morning beside a
> mountain stream,
> I seized a cloud from the sky above and
> fashioned myself a dream.
> In the hush of the early twilight, far from the
> haunts of men,

I wasted a summer evening, and fashioned
my dream again.
Wasted? Perhaps. Folks say so who never
have walked with God,
When lanes are purple with lilacs or yellow
with goldenrod.
But I have found strength for my labors in
that one short evening hour.
I have found joy and contentment; I have
found peace and power.
My dreaming has left me a treasure, a hope
that is strong and true.
From wasted hours I have built my life
and found my faith anew.

Going Deeper

1. Reread Psalm 5:1-3. Does this sound like some-
    one who has a surface or a deep relationship
    with God? Deep

2. Do you have a daily quiet time? Have you set
    aside periodic extended times to rebuild your
    relationship with God? If not, the wisest deci-
    sion you could make this week is to commit
    to a quiet time with God.
    No, No

Further Reading: Psalms 3:4; 84:3; 88:13.

Be Authentic

Do not merely listen to the word, and so deceive
yourselves. Do what it says.
Anyone who listens to the word but does not do what it says
is like a man who looks at his face in a mirror and,
after looking at himself,
goes away and immediately forgets what he looks like.
But the man who looks intently into the perfect law
that gives freedom,
and continues to do this, not forgetting what he
has heard, but doing it—
he will be blessed in what he does.

James 1:22-25

To make a difference in your world you have to be real.
There is nothing worse than a holier-than-thou Christian
who never shares his or her hurts and sorrows. I don't
know about you, but I can't relate to perfection. Authentic
people make a difference in the world.

I heard recently of a minister in the Midwest who was
going for a walk with a soap salesman in the community
who was a real skeptic toward Christianity. They were having quite an active debate while walking through the park.
The businessman was getting in some good jabs at the
inconsistency of Christians.

As they were walking through the park, the soap sales-man questioned the minister, "How can you say that Christianity works when even within the inner-city park you see derelicts of every kind, drugs and prostitutes? Then you have the problems of the family, war and disease, not to mention the negative problems of the world. How can you say that Christianity works? Just look around; it's not working."

They walked in silence for a few moments and then the minister turned to him and said, "You're a soap sales-man, right?"

"Yes, of course."

"Is it good soap?"

"It's the best soap on the market!"

The minister turned and pointed to a small child play-ing in the park who was covered with dirt and grime, and said, "This boy is dirty and filthy from the mud in the park; doesn't your soap help him?"

The salesman said, "Well, you've got to apply the soap."

The minister's response was, "So it is with the Chris-tian faith. You must apply the Christian faith in order for it to work."

Going Deeper

1. James 1:22-25 describes two courses of action a Christian can take: The first is to just listen

to the word and the second is to listen to the word and do it. Which course of action do you take most in your Christian walk? *The first*

2. Is your walk as strong as your talk? In what area of your life do you need to be more authentic?

No - worship, thoughts prayers

Further Reading: John 13:17; James 2:12.

Fellowship: A Necessary Ingredient

Let us consider how we may spur one another on toward love
and good deeds. Let us not give up meeting together, as some are
in the habit of doing, but let us encourage one another—
and all the more as you see the Day approaching.

Hebrews 10:24-25

The Bible calls the Church "the bride of Christ" (Revelation 19:7). God loves the Church, even with all of her inconsistencies. I honestly believe that you cannot be all God intends you to be without experiencing the intimate fellowship which the Church has to offer.

The Church is not a place for you to come, sit and be entertained. You are a part of the Church. You have a job. The Church is like a lifesaving station. The following story helps me get a better perspective of what the Church of Jesus Christ is all about and what my role in the Church should be.

On a dangerous seacoast where shipwrecks often occur, there was once a crude little lifesaving station. The building was just a hut and there was only one boat; but the few devoted members kept a constant watch over the sea, and with no thought for themselves went out day and night tirelessly searching for the lost. Some of those who were saved, and various others in the surrounding area, wanted to become associated with the station and give of their time and money and effort for the support of its work. New boats were bought and new crews trained. The little lifesaving station grew.

Some of the members of the lifesaving station were unhappy that the building was so crude and poorly equipped. They felt that a more comfortable place should be provided as the first refuge for those saved from the sea, so they replaced the emergency cots with beds and put better furniture in the enlarged building. Now the lifesaving station became a popular gathering place for its members, and they decorated it beautifully and furnished it exquisitely, because they used it as a sort of club. Fewer members were now interested in going to sea on lifesaving missions, so they hired lifeboat crews to do this work. The lifesaving motif still prevailed in this club's decoration, and there was a liturgical lifeboat in the room where the club initiations were held.

About this time a large ship was wrecked off the coast, and the hired crews brought in boatloads of cold, wet and half-drowned people. They were dirty and sick, and some of them had black skin and some had yellow skin. The beautiful new club was in chaos. So the property committee immediately had a shower house built outside the club where victims of a shipwreck could be cleaned up before coming inside.

At the next meeting, there was a split in the club membership. Most of the members wanted to stop the club's lifesaving activities as being unpleasant and a hindrance to the normal social life of the club. Some members insisted upon lifesaving as their primary purpose and pointed out that they were still called a lifesaving station. But the latter group were finally voted down and told that if they wanted to save the lives of all the various kinds of people who were shipwrecked in those waters, they could begin their own lifesaving station down the coast. They did.

As the years went by, the new station experienced the same changes that had occurred in the old. It evolved into a club, and yet another lifesaving station was founded. History continued to repeat itself, and if you visit that seacoast today, you will find a number of exclusive clubs along that shore. Shipwrecks are frequent in those waters, but most of the people drown.[18]

Going Deeper

1. Reread Hebrews 10:24-25. Have you given up meeting together with other Christians? *No*

2. Do you have the consistent fellowship you need to be a growing Christian? Would you consider yourself a participant in your church or a spectator? *Yes, Participant*

Further Reading: Acts 2:42; Hebrews 3:13.

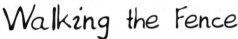

Walking the Fence

I know your deeds, that you are neither cold nor hot. I wish you were either one or the other! So, because you are lukewarm—neither hot nor cold—I am about to spit you out of my mouth.

Revelation 3:15-16

Everyone at one time or another has tried to keep his balance while walking on a fence. Sometimes we make it and sometimes we fall. When it comes to obedience, far too many Christians try to "walk the fence." They keep one foot in the Spirit while one foot flirts with the world. These are some of the unhappiest people in the world.

Charles Spurgeon once said, "I never saw anybody try to walk on both sides of the street but a drunken man; he tried it, and it was awkward work indeed; but I have seen many people in a moral point of view try to walk on both sides of the street, and I thought there was some kind of intoxication in them."

If God is God and Christ is our Savior, let us give our undivided attention and whole hearts to God. A lukewarm Christian never has the joy of knowing the fullness of God. Obedience is the key to real faith. This is real faith: believing and acting obediently regardless of circumstances.

Going Deeper

1. Read today's Scripture passage and define what it means to be hot, cold and lukewarm.
2. Are there areas of your life where you are walking the fence? Make a decision today to get off the fence and walk in obedience.

1-hot - on fire for God
cold- not a believer
1ukwarm - mix of both

2 - Yes

Further Reading: Romans 12:11.

Attempting the Impossible

During the fourth watch of the night Jesus went out to them,
walking on the lake. When the disciples saw him walking
on the lake, they were terrified.
"It's a ghost," they said, and cried out in fear.
But Jesus immediately said to them:
"Take courage! It is I. Don't be afraid."

"Lord, if it's you," Peter replied, "tell me to come to you on the water."

"Come," he said.

Then Peter got down out of the boat, walked on the water to Jesus.
But when he saw the wind, he was afraid and,
beginning to sink, cried out, "Lord, save me!"

Immediately Jesus reached out his hand and caught him.
"You of little faith," he said, "why did you doubt?"

And when they climbed into the boat, the wind died down.
Then those who were in the boat worshiped him, saying,
"Truly you are the Son of God."

Matthew 14:25-33

In this story Peter's lack of faith forced him to sink so that
Jesus had to save him, but Peter is to be commended for
stepping out of the boat and attempting to walk on the
water. You'll notice the other disciples were not exactly

fighting to join Peter! Living by faith sometimes means stepping out into the unknown and depending on God to carry us through.

I'm afraid that too many times I never step out of the boat, and in my comfortable lifestyle I miss out on the fullness of God. People who walk by faith aren't afraid to attempt the impossible. I hope you are a person who places your life in the hands of God and walks on the side of the impossible.

The words below by Dr. Carl Bates often remind me to keep away from the comfortable and attempt something greater than my ability.

> There came a time in my life when I earnestly prayed, "God I want Your power!" Time wore on and the power did not come. One day the burden was more than I could bear. "God, why haven't You answered that prayer?" God seemed to whisper back His simple reply, "With plans no bigger than yours, you don't need My power."[19]

Going Deeper

1. How does today's Bible passage challenge you to step out in faith? w/ thoughts
2. Are you willing to be included among those who step out in faith and depend on the power of God?
     Yes but it's hard

Further Reading: Daniel 10:12.

Dare to Dream

I can do everything through him who gives me strength.

Philippians 4:13

I once heard it said, "I would rather attempt something great and fail than attempt nothing and succeed." What dream is God placing in your heart? Don't sit back and wait for someone else to make a difference when you can be that person. The world doesn't need more armchair quarterbacks; the world needs people like you to get in the arena and give it everything you can! It was President Theodore Roosevelt who said:

> It is not the critic who counts; not the man who points out how the strong man stumbled or where the doer of deeds could have done them better. The credit belongs to the man who is actually in the arena; whose face is marred by dust and sweat and blood; who strives valiantly; who errs, and comes short again and again, because there is no effort without error and shortcoming; who does actually try to do the deed; who knows the great

enthusiasm, the great devotion, and spends himself in a worthy cause; who, at the worst, if he fails, at least fails while daring greatly.[20]

Our Lord plants a dream in everyone's heart. Most often the dreams are mighty, life-changing dreams with long-term positive results. Take your dream, then take the words of Paul, "I can do everything through him who gives me strength," and make a difference in this world!

Going Deeper

1. Write Philippians 4:13 on an index card and read it anytime your dreams are being challenged.
2. What dream has God planted in your heart? What decisions in your life do you need to make in order to bring that dream to reality?

2- College, sucess
    Financial decisions

Further Reading: 2 Corinthians 12:9.

Encouragement

Thursday

Reach Out and Touch Someone

Dear friends, let us love one another, for love comes from God.
Everyone who loves has been born of God and knows God.
Whoever does not love does not know God, because God is love.

1 John 4:7-8

I love this story and want to share it with you.

Ever feel like a frog? Frogs feel slow, low, ugly,
puffed, drooped, pooped. I know. One told me.
The frog feeling comes when you want to be bright
but feel dumb, when you want to share but are selfish, when you want to be thankful but feel resent-
ment, when you want to be great but are small,
when you want to care but are indifferent.

Yes, at one time or another each of us has found
himself on a lily pad floating down the great river of
life. Frightened and disgusted, we are too froggish
to budge. Once upon a time there was a frog. But he
really wasn't a frog. He was a prince who looked and
felt like a frog. A wicked witch had cast a spell on

him. Only the kiss of a beautiful maiden could save him. But since when do cute chicks kiss frogs? So there he sat, unkissed prince in frog form. But miracles happen. One day a beautiful maiden grabbed him up and gave him a big smack. Crash! Boom! Zap! There he was, a handsome prince. And you know the rest. They lived happily ever after.[21]

As a Christian you can be used by God to help change people. In your life, who is the frog who has the potential of becoming a prince or princess? Your touch has the power to begin a change in him or her. I don't think there is anything greater than being one of God's assistants and helping Him in His work of changing human beings. Don't miss the wonderful experience of servanthood!

Going Deeper

1. Where does today's Scripture tell us love comes from? God
2. Are you in the habit of kissing frogs? Is there someone you know who needs your love and attention? No, Yes

Further Reading: 1 John 2:4; 3:11.

Be Liberal with Encouragement

Encourage one another and build each other up,
just as in fact you are doing.

1 Thessalonians 5:11

Mark Twain once said, "I can live two months on one good compliment." People need your praise and affirmation. Be liberal with your gift of encouragement and always be on the lookout for opportunities to lift someone's spirits.

A woman in my church has a ministry of affirmation. She must have stock in the local stationery store because she is always writing affirming notes. I save those notes; I've received eight this year! Her willingness to praise someone for a job well done or encourage a person who needs a moment of inspiration has given my friend a profound ministry. She'll probably never give a sermon, write a book or be famous; but I guarantee you that in God's eyes, her notes of encouragement are more powerful than most sermons you've ever heard.

Is there someone in your life who needs a little affirmation and praise? What better gift to give him or her than the gift of encouragement!

Going Deeper

1. What effect does encouragement have in a person's life? Profound
2. Today give encouragement to someone who needs it. Try writing an uplifting note, giving a friendly phone call or baking a fresh batch of cookies for that person you would like to encourage.

Further Reading: Ephesians 4:29.

Your Smile Costs Nothing but Gives Much

A cheerful look brings joy to the heart, and good news gives health to the bones.

Proverbs 15:30

I will never understand all the good that a simple smile can accomplish.

Mother Teresa of Calcutta[22]

One of the greatest ways to love someone is to give him or her your smile. I have long forgotten where I found this profound thought, but I share it with you and challenge you to share your smile with someone else today:

A smile costs nothing, but gives much. It enriches those who receive, without making poorer those who give. It takes but a moment, but the memory of it sometimes lasts forever. None is so rich or mighty that he can get along without it, and none is so poor but that he can be made rich by it. Yet it cannot be bought, begged, borrowed or stolen, for it is something that is of no value to anyone until it is given away. Some people are too tired to give you a smile. Give them one of yours, as none needs a smile so much as he who has no more to give.

Going Deeper

1. God gave you your smile so that you could give it away. Sometimes God uses a simple smile to change the life of someone who needs it. Sometimes the first step of sharing your faith is your smile. Who needs your smile today?
2. A smile is an outward sign of an inward affection or love. Where does 1 John 4:7-8 say our inward love comes from?

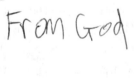

1- friends

From God

Further Reading: Psalm 67:1-2.

Sunday

The Adjustments of Love

My command is this: Love each other as I have loved you.
Greater love has no one than this, that he lay down
his life for his friends.

John 15:12-13

A surgeon wrote this story about an experience that changed his life:

I stand by the bed where a young woman lies, her face postoperative, her mouth twisted in palsy, clownish. A tiny twig of the facial nerve, the one to the muscles of her mouth, has been severed. She will be thus from now on. The surgeon had followed with religious fervor the curve of her flesh; I promise you that. Nevertheless, to remove the tumor in her cheek, I had cut the little nerve. Her young husband is in the room. He stands on the opposite side of the bed, and together they seem to dwell in the evening lamplight, isolated from me, private. *Who are they,* I ask myself, *he and this wry mouth I have made, who gaze at and touch each other so generously, greedily?*

The young woman speaks. "Will my mouth always be like this?"

"Yes," I say, "it will. It is because the nerve was cut." She nods and is silent.

But the young man smiles. "I like it," he says. "It is kind of cute."

All at once I know who he is. I understand, and lower my gaze. One is not bold in an encounter with a great man. Unmindful, he bends to kiss her crooked mouth, and I am so close I can see how he twists his own lips to accommodate to hers, to show her that their kiss still works.[23]

This husband was a great man. In the midst of what could have been a horrible experience for all, he rose above his shock: He accommodated his life and kiss to set his wife at ease.

As a Christian you are called to adjust your life to serve your fellow human beings. What is God calling you to do with your life? Are you willing to follow His call? Are you willing to make some adjustments to your lifestyle if necessary?

Going Deeper

1. What does Jesus call us to do in John 15:12-13? *love*
2. What can you do with your life to make it count? Is there a part of your life that you've been complaining about that really would be better off if

you took a different attitude about it? Today
make an accommodation of love that you've
needed to make for a long time.

⌐ Yes
⌐ Dedicate it
to God.

Actions Speak Louder Than Words

Dear children, let us not love with words or tongue
but with actions and in truth.

1 John 3:18

Your actions will speak much louder than any words you will ever say. When you call yourself a Christian, you are opening your life up for inspection, and your life becomes an active witness for Jesus Christ. The positive news is that people will respond to your good deeds and thoughtful acts of caring. In fact, people will want to know more about the Savior you love, as your deeds prove to them that your faith is more walk than talk. Here's a story with an important message:

Shortly after World War II came to a close, Europe began picking up the pieces. Much of the Old Country had been ravaged by war and was in ruins. Perhaps the saddest sight of all was that of little orphaned children starving in the streets of those war-torn cities.

Early one chilly morning an American soldier was making his way back to the barracks in London.

As he turned the corner in his jeep, he spotted a little lad with his nose pressed to the window of a pastry shop. Inside the cook was kneading dough for a fresh batch of doughnuts. The hungry boy stared in silence, watching every move. The soldier pulled his jeep to the curb, stopped, got out, and walked quietly over to where the little fellow was standing. Through the steamed window he could see the mouthwatering morsels as they were being pulled from the oven, piping hot. The boy salivated and released a slight groan as he watched the cook place them onto the glass-enclosed counter ever so carefully.

The soldier's heart went out to the nameless orphan as he stood beside him. "Son . . . would you like some of those?" The boy was startled.

"Oh, yeah . . . I would!"

The American stepped inside and bought a dozen, put them in a bag, and walked back to where the lad was standing in the foggy cold of the London morning. He smiled, held out the bag, and said simply: "Here you are."

As he turned to walk away, he felt a tug on his coat. He looked back and heard the child ask quietly: "Mister . . . are you God?"

We are never more like God than when we give. "God so loved the world, that He gave . . ."[24]

Going Deeper

1. Words can be powerful, but how much more powerful can they be if they are backed up with actions?
2. What act of kindness or gift of love can you give to someone today? Is your lifestyle representing Jesus in a positive manner with your deeds?

nice to bro,N.

Further Reading: Ezekiel 33:31; Romans 12:9; 1 John 2:1.

Tuesday

Friendship:
A Priceless Gift

A friend loves at all times.

Proverbs 17:17

Faithful friends are a sturdy shelter:
whoever finds one has found a treasure.
Faithful friends are beyond price:
no amount can balance their worth.
Faithful friends are life-saving medicine:
and those who fear the Lord will find them.

Sirach 6:14-16

There are very few things in life as important or as wonderful as true friendship. A good friend is a treasure beyond almost anything else in life. Friendship is a priceless gift from God. Iverson Williams once wrote:

Friendship is a special blessing from above. It's sharing of activities with someone who understands and cares. It's a warm ray of sunshine that fills our hearts in times of need. It's bringing out of beautiful things in each other that no one else looked hard enough to find. It's the mutual trust and honesty that lets us be ourselves at all times.

Going Deeper

1. What characteristic of friendship is described in Proverbs 17:17? loyalty
2. How can you deepen your friendships today? What words can you say or what actions can you take to insure your friends know you love them? Finding believing friends, tell them

Further Reading: 2 Samuel 15:21.

I Stand by the Door

I am the door; if any one enters by me, he will be saved,
and will go in and out and find pasture.

John 10:9, RSV

Sam Shoemaker spent his life helping people find new life and meaning in Jesus Christ. He had a special love for those who had never made a commitment to Jesus Christ. One day he sat down to write his philosophy of life and he penned this work of prose:

I stand by the door.
I neither go too far in, nor stay too far out.
The door is the most important door in the world—
It is the door through which men walk when they find God.
There's no use my going way inside, and staying there,
When so many are still outside and they, as much as I,
Crave to know where the door is.
And all that so many ever find
Is only the wall where a door ought to be.
They creep along the wall like blind men,
With outstretched, groping hands.
Feeling for a door, knowing there must be a door,

Yet they never find it . . .
So I stand by the door.
The most tremendous thing in the world
Is for men to find that door—the door to God.[25]

Do you know someone who needs to be introduced to the new life that Jesus Christ offers? Maybe you are the one to introduce her or him to your Lord. Since I know that in Christ people can find new life, why am I so shy about introducing them to the *source* of new life? If I really love them, I'll give them the same opportunity to come in the door and meet the Master that I have had. How about you? Is it time to hang around the door and make some introductions?

Going Deeper

1. Who do you know who needs to be introduced to Jesus Christ? What's keeping you from helping them meet? Quinn, pressure

2. Reread Sam Shoemaker's thoughts and then pray for an opportunity to do some introducing!

Further Reading: Acts 3:1-10.

Thursday
Apr. 5!!

Make Me an Instrument

> He said to his disciples, "The harvest is plentiful
> but the workers are few."
>
> Matthew 9:37

Francis of Assisi was a wealthy, highborn man who lived hundreds of years ago. He felt that his life was incomplete; even though he had more than enough wealth, he was a very unhappy man. One day while he was out riding, he met a leper. The leper was loathsome and repulsive in the ugliness of his disease. Something moved Francis to dismount and fling his arms around this person. In the arms of Francis, the leper's face changed to the face of Christ. Francis was never the same again.

Francis of Assisi spent the rest of his life serving his Lord Jesus Christ. He wrote these famous words as a prayer to God from the heart of a man who had a deep desire to be an instrument of God's will on this earth. Lord, make me an instrument of Your peace.

> Where there is hatred, let me sow love;
> where there is injury, pardon;
> where there is doubt, faith;

where there is despair, hope;
where there is darkness, light;
and where there is sadness joy.[26]

Going Deeper

1. Matthew 9:37 tells us there are many people who still need to know the peace, love, faith, hope, light and joy of Jesus Christ. Are you willing to put in the work necessary to tell these people about Jesus?
2. How does it make you feel to know that God wants to use you as an instrument of peace?

Important

Further Reading: Luke 10:2; John 4:35.

Endnotes

1. *Ideas Books #1720* (El Cajon, CA: Youth Specialties, 1976), p. 151.
2. Jim Burns, *Handling Your Hormones: The Straight Scoop on Love and Sexuality* (Eugene, OR: Harvest House, 1986), pp. 46-47.
3. Tim Hansel, *You Gotta Keep Dancin'* (Elgin, IL: David C. Cook, 1985), pp. 16-17.
4. Charles Colson, *Loving God* (Grand Rapids, MI: Zondervan Publishing House, 1983), p. 176.
5. Clarence Jordan, *Sermon on the Mount* (Valley Forge, PA: Judson Press, 1970), pp. 59-60.
6. John Newton, "Amazing Grace," first published in *Olney Hymns* (London: W. Oliver, 1779), cited at *cyberhymnal.org*. http://www.cyberhymnal.org/htm/a/m/amazgrac.htm (accessed August 2006).
7. Randy Stonehill, *Celebrate This Heartbeat* (Waco, TX: Word Records, Inc., 1984).
8. Ideas taken from *Crossroads* of the First Christian Church (June 11, 1978), n.p.
9. Ted W. Engstrom, *The Pursuit of Excellence* (Grand Rapids, MI: Zondervan Publishing House, 1982), p. 90. Used by permission.
10. Leo Buscaglia, *Living, Loving and Learning* (New York: Random House, 1982), p. 153.
11. Poem by an unknown confederate soldier, quoted in Tim Hansel, *When I Relax I Feel Guilty* (Elgin, IL: David C. Cook, 1979), p. 89.
12. Charles Paul Conn, quoted in Ted W. Engstrom, *The Pursuit of Excellence* (Grand Rapids, MI: Zondervan Publishing House, 1982), p. 21.
13. Carolyn Carty, "Footprints," written in 1963.
14. Ted W. Engstrom, *The Pursuit of Excellence* (Grand Rapids, MI: Zondervan Publishing House, 1982), p. 57.
14. Søren Kierkegaard, quoted in Tony Campolo, *You Can Make a Difference* (Waco, TX: Word Publishing, 1984), p. 74.
16. John Cateior, ed., *What a Day This Can Be* (London: Darton, Longman and Todd, Ltd., 1966), n.p.
17. Margery Williams, *The Velveteen Rabbit* (New York: Avon Books, 1975), pp. 16-17.
18. *Ideas Books #58* (El Cajon, CA: Youth Specialties, 1970), pp. 78-79.
19. Dr. Carl Bates, quoted in Bill Glass, *Expect to Win* (Waco, TX: Word Publishing, 1981), p. 52.
20. Theodore Roosevelt, quoted in Ted W. Engstrom, *The Pursuit of Excellence* (Grand Rapids, MI: Zondervan Publishing House, 1982), p. 57.
21. Wes Seeliger, quoted in Bruce Larson, *Ask Me to Dance* (Waco, TX: Word Publishing, 1972), p. 11.

22. Mother Teresa of Calcutta, quoted in José Luis González-Balado, *Mother Teresa: In My Own Words* (New York: Gramercy Books, 1996), p. 75.

23. Dr. Richard Selzer, "The Kiss," *Parable* (January 1983), p. 3.

24. Charles Swindoll, *Improving Your Serve* (Waco, TX: Word Publishing, 1981), pp. 52-53.

25. Sam Shoemaker, preface to *I Stand by the Door* by Helen Smith Shoemaker (Waco, TX: Word Publishing, 1978).

26. Francis of Assisi (1181–1226), "Prayer of St. Francis."

You Only Have One Life—
Make It Count for God!

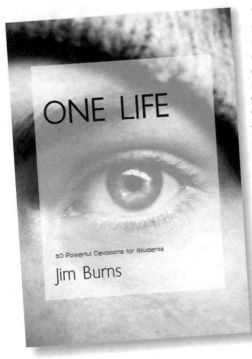

When was the last time you spent with God? Get started now with these 50 fresh devotional readings that cover many of the major issues of life and faith you're wrestling with. Sexual purity, the pressure to compromise, family relationships, trusting God, servanthood, worry, burnout and daily surrender are just a few of the topics you'll dig into. Interesting stories illustrate each devotional reading, making the issues come alive. You'll dive deeper into Scripture and find plenty of application questions to help you make changes in your own journey of faith. It's also perfect for you and your friends to do together. You only have one life, so why not discover the greatest adventure life has to offer?

One Life
50 Powerful Devotions for Students
ISBN 08307.43049

Available at Bookstores Everywhere!

Visit **www.regalbooks.com** to join **Regal's FREE e-newsletter.**
You'll get useful **excerpts from our newest releases** and **special
access to online chats with your favorite authors.** Sign up today!

Regal
God's Word for Your World™
www.regalbooks.com